NAPOLEON BONAPARTE

The Emperor of France

Written by Hadrien Nafilyan
Translated by Jessica Foster

NAPOLEON BONAPARTE

KEY INFORMATION

- **Born:** 15 August 1769 in Ajaccio (Corsica).
- **Died:** 5 May 1821 on Saint Helena (British island in the South Atlantic Ocean).
- **Main achievements:** while trying to establish a compromise between the Ancien Régime and the fundamental achievements of the French Revolution (1789), he laid the groundwork for the contemporary world.

INTRODUCTION

There are similarities between the beginning and end of Napoleon's life: he was born on an island under Bourbon reign, and he died on another island ruled over by another Bourbon king. However, between those two events he was to change the face of Europe, and practically of the world, following a rapid ascension which in just ten years led him to military, political and administrative domination of an entire continent.

A general during the Revolution at the age of 26, head of government at 30, Emperor at 35: this extraordinary fate for a man from a modest background can certainly be explained by his exceptional qualities, but also by the national and international context of his time. He arrived on the scene in the early 1800s as the saviour of the Revolution, and to secure it from both internal enemies (fierce royalists and uncompromising republicans) and external enemies

(Austria, Russia, Prussia and above all Britain), he had no other choice but to seize power, with the support of the majority of French citizens.

He had to tread a fine line and make a series of decisions aimed at placating the royalists – by implementing the Concordat and granting amnesty to *émigrés* (French aristocrats who had fled following the Revolution) – and at satisfying the republicans – by safeguarding the achievements of the Revolution, whether they were civic, such as equality, or territorial, such as Belgium. He also had to silence any opposition, by executing the Duke of Enghien on the one hand and by eliminating the power of the assemblies on the other. Lastly, he needed to participate in wars with increasing economic, financial and human costs.

In short, Napoleon was unremittingly devoted to establishing and maintaining peace, both outside and inside the borders of his state. His raison d'être began with peace. The French were grateful to him for putting an end to ten years of anarchy and internal divisions, and the European peace treaties he signed were always warmly welcomed by the public. Peace also enabled him to build and reform the country, notably by establishing the civil institutions, such as the Bank of France, on which France still relies today. Napoleon was at least as much an administrator as he was a conqueror.

Unlike a monarch from an established dynasty, or a president whose power is secured by institutions, Napoleon never had any legitimacy other than that which he created for himself. This legitimacy, despite his best efforts to embed it in history, would still remain fragile in the eyes of the French population, and would never be recognised by European monarchies, who would continue to fight him until his eventual downfall.

THE LIFE OF NAPOLEON BONAPARTE

A CHILDHOOD IN CORSICA

Napoleon Bonaparte was born on 15 August 1769 in Ajaccio, Corsica, when the island had just been annexed by France (1768), to a family of the lower nobility, well-off without being rich. His father, re-allied to the French party, was a lawyer for the Council of the Twelve Nobles of Dila then made Deputy of the Nobility of Corsica in 1777. Napoleon went to the continent for the first time in 1778 to begin his military training, first at the royal academy in Brienne, then at the *École Militaire* in Paris, from where he graduated as an artillery officer in 1785. He was an excellent pupil throughout his studies, but had a melancholy and solitary temperament.

NAPOLEON'S FAMILY

Eight of the fourteen children of Carlo Buonaparte (1746-1785) and Maria Letizia Ramolino (1750-1836) survived. Joseph (1767-1844), future King of Naples and of Spain, was the oldest and Napoleon the second, followed by Lucien (1775-1840), Elisa (1777-1820), Grand Duchess of Tuscany, Louis (1778-1846), future King of Holland, Pauline (1780-1825), Caroline (1782-1839), Queen of Naples and wife of Joachim Murat (1767-1815), and finally Jérôme (1784-1860), future King of Westphalia. The family were sometimes unruly and troublesome for Napoleon, but he used them to cement his power by placing them on the thrones of European monarchies.

From 1785 to 1793, Napoleon, despite being a French officer, was completely focused on Corsica, as he saw his future there. As he was anti-French at this point, he became involved with Pasquale Paoli (1725-1807), leader of the party of patriots who were against French occupation, whom he would break from in 1793 when Paoli became too counterrevolutionary for his liking. From 1789 to 1793, due to military leave of absence and dismissal, he spent the equivalent of three years in Corsica, and thus missed the Revolution that was happening in the capital.

<u>DID YOU KNOW?</u>

Napoleon initially wanted to become a writer. He wrote a book on the history of Corsica when he was young, as well as two or three works of fiction, including *Clisson et Eugénie*. He would maintain this passion for writing throughout his life.

HIS ASCENSION

He managed to rejoin national history when, after being forced to flee Corsica with his family, he recommenced service in the revolutionary armies, for both financial and ideological reasons. He was first noticed during the Siege of Toulon, taken back from the British in December 1793, but it was his suppression of the royalist insurrection in Paris in October 1795 (13 Vendémiaire) which marked the real turning point in his career. General Vendémiaire, as he was nicknamed, then frequented high society, where he met Joséphine (1763-1814), the widow of Alexandre de Beauharnais (1760-1794), whom he married in March 1796, at the age of 27.

Watercolour by Berthault depicting the attack on the National Convention of 13 Vendémiaire Year 4.

The victories of the First Italian Campaign (1796-1797) against Austria and the Treaty of Campo Formio that resulted from it played a key role in young Napoleon's glory, and he was elected to the *Institut de France* on 25 December 1796. Worried about his high status, the Directory sent him to Egypt (1798-1799) with the aim of blocking the route to the Indies from the British. The campaign failed, but Napoleon paradoxically gained power and fame from it: its exoticism and the successful scientific results of the voyage would be remembered. When he returned, the great political instability that rocked Paris at the time gave him an opportunity to seize power.

CULMINATION

The coup d'état of 18 Brumaire (9 November 1799) marked the beginning of the Napoleonic saga. Having been made First Consul in 1800, then Consul for Life in 1802, he was crowned Emperor on 2 December 1804. Until 1808, his power knew no limits. He conquered the various coalitions created to fight him, notably by Britain, Austria, Russia and Prussia, and gradually annexed a large area of Europe. Keen to defeat Britain, he launched a decree for a continental blockade in 1806, a crucial system in the fight against the island.

Napoleon was also a great reformer. As well as the institutions, in 1801 he established the Concordat, which re-established links between France and the papacy and proclaimed religious freedom. At the same time, he managed to fix the country's finances and economy by establishing a stable currency, the *franc germinal*.

However, for many people, he went too far when he created the titles of nobility of the First French Empire in 1808, married Marie Louise of Austria (1791-1847), the great-niece of Marie-Antoinette (1755-1793), in 1810, and held Pope Pius VII (1742-1823) captive from 1809 to 1813 to force him to close the Papal States to British trade.

DOWNFALL

From 1808 onwards, the fate of the Empire took a turn for the worse. Initially, there was the rut caused by the military situation in Spain, which Napoleon was occupying to defend his territory from the British, who were trying to defy the blockade, then the resuming of the war with the Allies, which culminated in 1812 with the disastrous Russian Campaign. Gradually the Allies won back the territories conquered by France, until they arrived at the gates of Paris in March 1814. After bidding farewell to his Old Guard, he abdicated on 6 April 1814 at Fontainebleau. A few days later, he tried to poison himself.

He was exiled to the island of Elba (Italian island on the Tyrrhenian Sea), where he was authorised to reign under his title of Emperor, but from where he fled on 26 February 1815 to regain power in Paris, taking advantage of the discontent caused by Louis XVIII's (1755-1824) return to the throne. Thus began the Hundred Days period, during which Napoleon summoned the country's last strength, and which ended with a second abdication on 22 June, four days after their defeat at Waterloo by the Allies.

Napoleon leaving Elba, on 26 February 1815, painting by Joseph Beaume, 1836.

He briefly hoped to seek refuge in America but, refusing to flee, he handed himself over to the British who deported him to Saint Helena, where he died in 1821 after six years in captivity. It was not until 1840 that Louis Philippe had his remains repatriated to France in a grand ceremony, and buried them at the Hôtel des Invalides, where they remain to this day.

Napoleon's death

The doctors who performed the autopsy on Napoleon's body in the days following his death attributed it to stomach cancer. Modern researchers, after analysing the various reports from the autopsy, lean more towards the hypothesis of an aggravated gastric ulcer. Conversely, the theory of arsenic poisoning, which has also been suggested, has been refuted by most historians.

CONTEXT

CORSICA

In 1768, Corsica was sold to France by the Republic of Genoa, which had dominated the island since the 14th century, but was now unable to suppress the rebellions of Corsican nationalists led by Pasquale Paoli. The patriots were defeated once and for all by French troops two months before Napoleon was born. Corsica was thus divided into two rival factions: those in favour of annexation by France, including Carlo Buonaparte, and the pro-Paoli separatists, to whom Napoleon would become close. The separatists split during the Reign of Terror (1792-1794) between those in favour of Britain and those in favour of the National Convention (French revolutionary government). Paoli preferred the former, Napoleon the latter, hence their split and the Bonaparte family's escape to the continent. Paoli entrusted Corsica to the British until it was recaptured by the Italian army in April 1796.

THE FIRST COALITION (1792-1797)

Initially moderate in its principles and views, the Revolution accelerated from 1792 onwards, with France proving itself aggressive towards neighbouring monarchies. The abolition of the constitutional monarchy in September 1792, the beheading of Louis XVI on 21 January 1793 and the expansionist leanings of the revolutionaries aggravated the situation considerably, which would lead to the First Coalition formed by Austria, the Kingdom of Piedmont-Sardinia and

Great Britain, among others. Faced with this threat, the Revolution mobilised all the nation's resources. This was the context when Napoleon arrived on the continent and rid Toulon of the British, then led his First Italian Campaign against Austria and signed the Treaty of Campo Formio, which put an end to the First Coalition on 18 October 1797.

EUROPEAN POWERS AT THE END OF THE 18TH CENTURY

Other than France, there were five large state entities in Europe at the end of the 18th century, starting with those ruled by the House of Habsburg, then represented by Francis II (1768-1835). This was the Holy Roman Empire, which was formed of many small states that roughly correspond to modern-day Germany, the Czech Republic, Belgium, Northern Italy and Hungary. The other main powers were Great Britain, Russia – where Paul I (1754-1801) reigned, followed by Alexander I (1777-1825) – Spain and Prussia, initially part of the Holy Roman Empire but which the conquests of Frederick II (1712-1786) had extended to Poland and modern-day Lithuania.

As well as these five major entities, there was the Dutch Republic, made up of part of the modern-day Netherlands; the Kingdom of the Two Sicilies, run by the Bourbons, made up of Southern Italy and Sicily; the Papal States of central Italy; the Kingdom of Sardinia, which included the island itself and the Italian Piedmont; and finally Portugal and Switzerland.

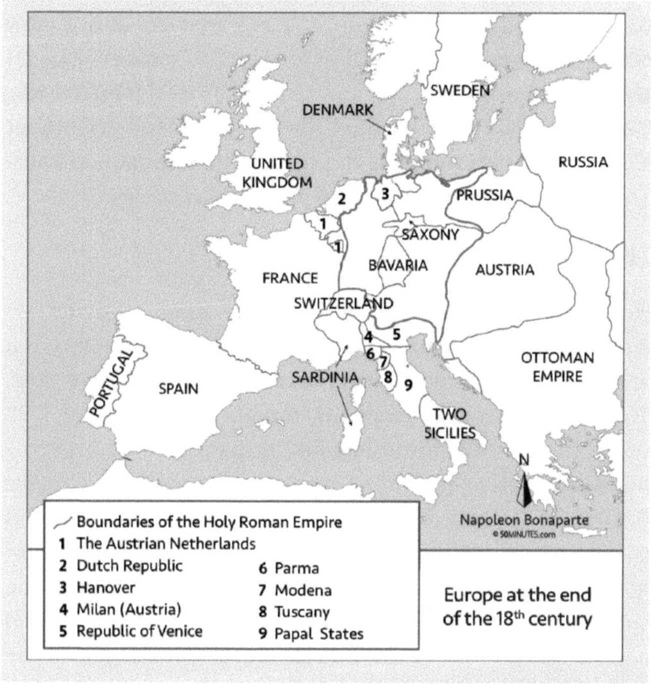

THE FIRST REPUBLIC (1792-1799)

Napoleon made his military début during the Reign of Terror, an episode of the Revolution in which the Convention, dominated by the Jacobins (republican extremists), perpetrated mass killings and made many arbitrary decisions. This troubled period ended on 28 July 1794 with the execution of the most radical fringe of the Jacobins, which Maximilien Robespierre (1758-1794) and his brother Augustin (1763-1794), a friend of Napoleon, were part of. After an attempt to develop the Convention, it was removed and a new constitution instated the Directory on 26 October 1795. Of the five directors then inaugurated, the most significant was Paul Barras (1755-1829), who called on Napoleon in October 1795 to help him suppress the royalist insurrection in Paris. The young general then moved in powerful circles.

The 18 Brumaire coup d'état

However, this form of government soon showed its weaknesses and its inability to defend itself against internal enemies (essentially royalists) and external enemies alike. The Second Coalition was put in place at the end of 1798 when the First Coalition had just disbanded, and caused a number of setbacks for the Directory. It thus seemed urgent for one of its last directors, Emmanuel Sieyès (1748-1836) to announce a new constitution establishing a stronger government. To help him with this process, he needed the support of a military man and chose Napoleon, who had just returned from Egypt. But the general managed to use the coup d'état, which took place on 18 Brumaire, Year VIII (9 November 1799), to his advantage: the other two Consuls, Jean Jacques de Cambacérès (1753-1824) and Charles François Lebrun (1739-1824) were made subordinate to him.

Bonaparte at the Council of Five Hundred, in Saint-Cloud, on 10 November 1799, painting by François Bouchot, 1840.

THE SITUATION IN 1800

When Napoleon became head of the Consulate established in the Constitution of the Year VIII, France was exhausted following ten years of revolution and civil and foreign wars, to the extent that nobody opposed his takeover, which happened without violence. Conversely, people were happy to see the return of authority, the only thing capable of establishing peace across the territory, fighting robbery and leading an effective war against the Allies. Additionally, the economic situation was very bad and there was a financial crisis. The Directory implemented a series of reforms, whose results would be felt under the Consulate and whose rewards Napoleon would reap.

Above all, the future of the Revolution was at stake. The monarchists threatened to overthrow a now fragile republic. The political elite, still mostly made up of revolutionary assemblies and the majority of which had voted in favour of the death of Louis XVI, feared the revenge that the return of the monarchy would bring. The revolutionary middle classes were afraid of seeing freedom, equality or the elimination of corporations compromised. Meanwhile, the beneficiaries of the sale of national treasures, the possessions of the Church and the aristocracy confiscated by the Revolution, who were mostly peasants, were worried about having to give these things back to their original owners. Most French citizens therefore eagerly awaited the confirmation of the fundamental achievements of the Revolution and the establishment of a strong government, capable of protecting them.

FRANCE ALONE AGAINST THE WORLD

The various states under French imperial rule did not have the same status: there was a distinction between countries that were dependent but that kept a certain autonomy, and the annexed territories that had fully become French departments. This was the case for Belgium and all the states located on the left bank of the Rhine. These new departments, conquered by the National Convention starting in 1792, were made inalienable by the Constitution of the Year VIII, which stipulated that the Republic was whole and indivisible, and Napoleon committed to keeping the Revolution's territorial heritage intact.

However, for political and economic reasons, the annexation of Belgium by France was unacceptable to Britain, who refused any attempts at peace and continued to form various alliances. After being defeated several times, their allies on land were ready to surrender to Napoleon, but Britain relaunched the offensive each time. Napoleon knew that there could be no stable peace until Great Britain was defeated. All his policies therefore aimed to defeat them. Rejecting the idea of a marine attack, which had been rendered impossible following the destruction of the French fleet at Trafalgar on 21 October 1805, he set up a continental blockade, aimed at stifling the British economy. It was with the aim of extending the blockade that he tried to establish alliance treaties or conquer the states on the Atlantic and Mediterranean shores. Finally, it was also to fight Britain that he ventured into Spain and Portugal and launched the Russian Campaign.

In 1802, Napoleon decided to send an expedition to the Dominican Republic, firstly to re-establish French authority which had been jeopardised by the slaves' revolt, led by Toussaint Louverture (1743-1803), and secondly to serve as a base for the occupation of Louisiana, which had been given back to France by Spain in 1800. However, when the expedition failed, Napoleon gave up on American politics and sold Louisiana to the United States in 1803. Franco-American relations remained frosty throughout the period: the Americans were unhappy about the downfall of the French monarchy and were penalised by the continental blockade, while the French did not allow the United States to continue to trade with their rebelling colonies or with Britain. In South America, all of Napoleon's efforts would aim to ensure that Spain's old rebel colonies did not fall into British hands.

BACK TO NORMAL

After Napoleon's downfall in 1814, and even more so in 1815, Europe seemed to regain the political balance it had lost after the French Revolution. However, during the Congress of Vienna which ended on 9 June 1815, the conquerors divided Europe between them according to borders which were slightly different from those that existed in 1789 and played to the advantage of Prussia, Austria and Russia.

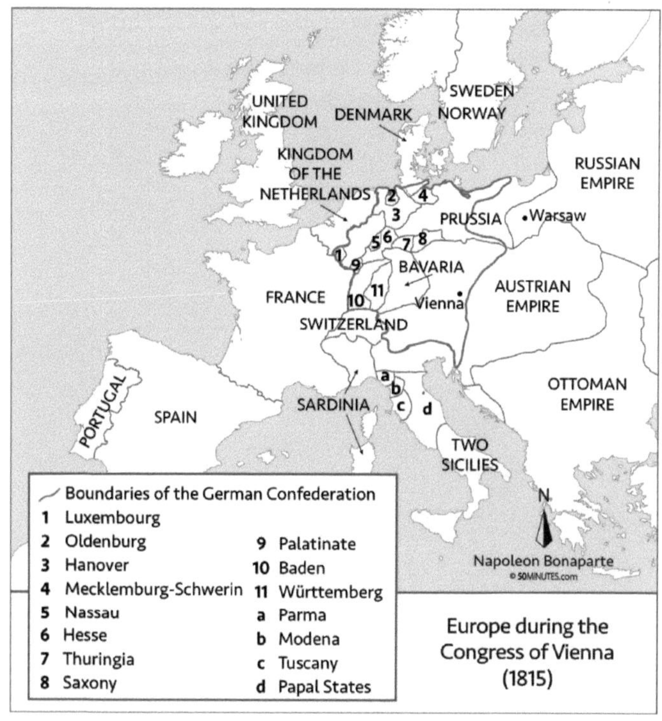

Europe during the
Congress of Vienna
(1815)

In France the monarchy was re-established, not without hostility, under a constitutional form which played to Louis XVIII's advantage. The Bourbon Restoration was initially set on a liberal path but, under pressure from the ultra-royalists (monarchists in favour of returning to the Ancien Régime without concessions), it took an increasingly regressive path. However, exiled to the middle of nowhere, Napoleon was no longer concerned by these events. The man who had created the global historical context in which he had evolved was now completely on the sidelines of history.

HIGHLIGHTS

GENERAL BONAPARTE

The First Italian Campaign (1796-1797)

Faced with the First Coalition, the Directory decided to attack Austria. While Generals Jourdan (1762-1833) and Moreau (1763-1813) passed through Germany, General Bonaparte was entrusted with the 50 000 men in the Italian army, whom he joined in March 1796. The campaign was an overwhelming success, and Napoleon went from victory to victory. On 10 May 1796, he won the Battle of Lodi, which opened the gates of Milan to him. Just as renowned is the Battle of Arcole, which took place between 15 and 17 November 1796, and during which Napoleon committed an act of bravery by crossing the bridge in front of his troops. The campaign ended with the Treaty of Campo Formio, signed with Austria on 18 October 1797.

The Battle of Lodi, painting by Louis-François Lejeune, 1804.

It was during this first campaign as an army general that Napoleon showed signs that he had the qualities which would lead to his military success: an authority to impose on officers, the ability to earn loyalty from soldiers through the attention he paid to them and his temperament, a full knowledge of how operations played out that left little to chance, and a tactic based on offensive action and quick movements which he used to surprise the enemy. He turned up where he was not expected and, in order to control as much space as possible, skilfully divided his troops – rarely by more than a day's walking so that they could come together in case they ran into the enemy and defeat them completely. The fact that he got rid of supplies and had his army live off the countries they passed through made this great mobility possible.

As well as his victories, the good fortune of Napoleon's exploits is largely due to the way he knew how to value them, especially among his soldiers. He created several newspapers for their use which he handed out for free and in which his acts were glorified and his personality exalted, in a style that sometimes even raised them to legendary status. These papers, which he often wrote himself, were indirectly intended for France, where they were also widely distributed. Bonaparte would show this flair for propaganda throughout his career.

The Egyptian expedition (1798-1799)

The official aim of the French campaign in Egypt was to cut off the British route to the Indies, and to increase France's economic resources. But it was also a way for the Directory to keep away a general whose glory, which he had acquired during the Italian Campaign, constituted a threat. However, it was Napoleon himself who suggested the expedition. He saw it as an opportunity to further increase his prestige through distant conquests made in the legendary East, already imagining himself going to Constantinople and even following in the footsteps of Alexander the Great (356-323 BC) to the Indies.

Additionally, in the same way as the Macedonian prince, Napoleon surrounded himself with the most distinguished scholars. The war campaign thus doubled up as a scientific expedition, whose considerable impact would help people to forget the military failures, to the extent that the events in Egypt would be remembered as a success for the nation. In summer 1798, he founded the *Institut d'Égypte* in Cairo, whose members assembled their works in the monumental *Description de l'Égypte*, published between 1809 and 1818. It was during this expedition that the Rosetta Stone was discovered, which would enable Jean-François Champollion (1790-1832) to decipher hieroglyphs in 1821.

THE MEMBERS OF THE EGYPTIAN EXPEDITION

Among the 167 scholars and artists from 18 specialities (with Napoleon himself even joining as a geometrician), there were, among others, mathematicians, chemists, astronomers, naturalists, geographers, engineers, architects, designers, printers, literary experts, a sculptor and even a pianist. Some members were well-known, such as the mathematician Gaspard Monge (1746-1818), the chemists Claude Berthollet (1748-1822) and Nicolas-Jacques Conté (1755-1805), the inventor of the Conté crayon, the naturalist Étienne Geoffroy Saint-Hilaire (1772-1844) and the designers Pierre-Joseph Redouté (1759-1840) and Vivant Denon (1747-1825). The poet François-Auguste Parseval-Grandmaison (1759-1834) was in charge of singing about the expedition's exploits.

The Mediterranean crossing went without a hitch, although the British fleet, under the orders of Admiral Horatio Nelson (1758-1805), tried to intercept the French ships. The island of

Malta was conquered on the way, and the expedition landed at Alexandria on 1 July 1798. The city was taken easily. Egypt was then an Ottoman province, controlled by the Mamluks, against whom the Battle of the Pyramids was waged on 21 July 1798. It was during his speech before the battle that Napoleon reportedly said the famous phrase, "From the heights of these pyramids, forty centuries look down on us." The tactical and technical superiority of the French made the difference, despite very trying weather conditions, and Napoleon seized Cairo, where he set up his headquarters.

Painting depicting the Battle of the Pyramids.

The destruction of the French ships by the British fleet in the Abu Qir Bay on 2 August 1798 quickly soured the mood. The French army, now cut off from their homeland, had to deal with illness, the hostility of the natives, who revolted in Cairo on 21 October 1798, and the Turks' waging war on them all alone. Napoleon took on the Turks, defeated them in Gaza, seized the town of Jaffa on 7 March 1799, then besieged Acre (then in Syria). After eight unsuccessful attacks, he lifted the siege in May 1799. He had to return to Egypt urgently to prevent the Turks from landing at Abu Qir. This battle resulted in a victory for him, but it was not enough to change the opinion of the French who, partly brainwashed by British propaganda, decried Napoleon's actions. He therefore decided to return to Paris as quickly as possible to defend himself, and secretly left Egypt on 23 August 1799, abandoning his army, which he had entrusted to Jean-Baptiste Kléber (1753-1800).

The French Campaign in Egypt alone sums up Napoleon. It firstly revealed the extent of the ambitions of a man who was no longer afraid to compare himself with Alexander the Great, but who nonetheless avoided all dogmatism. This lack of ideology led him to respect the beliefs and customs of the countries he occupied and even to encourage them to unite with the invading population, to the point that he once contemplated converting to Islam. This pragmatism, in its most extreme form bypassed any hesitation. This is why he did not think twice about massacring 3000 Turkish prisoners, as he had nothing to feed them with, nor about poisoning dozens of his own soldiers who had caught the plague in Jaffa, so that they would not cause further problems for him. His own interests, which he often confused with France's interests, came before any other consideration; in his mind, abandoning his army in Egypt, and later in Russia, was justified. Finally, it was during this campaign that he showed his ability to direct and manage a state, a quality that he would soon use to his advantage in France.

THE CONSUL

The era of great reform

During the four years of the Consulate (1799-1804), established following the coup d'état of 18 Brumaire, Napoleon undertook large-scale institutional reforms that marked his reign. This was the era of the new institutions: the Council of State (founded in 1799), the prefects (1800), the Bank of France (1800), schools for higher education (1802), the National Order of the Legion of Honour (1802), the *franc germinal* (1803), and above all the Napoleonic Code, passed in 1804.

The Napoleonic Code, or the Civil Code, which is still enforced today, although partially reworked, was the spearhead of Napoleon's policies, and he even imposed it on the annexed territories. Its main principles, notably the rule of the patriarchate and the defence of private property, met the expectations of the conservative middle class and some of the lower class. The Napoleonic Code finally brought rules to a country that had been governed by anarchy for ten years.

DID YOU KNOW?

Napoleon Bonaparte was a tireless worker. He usually only slept between four and five hours a night, but he could go for two days without sleep when he was on a campaign. Believing meals to be a waste of time, he ate in just 15 minutes. He met with council after council, gave command after command, showed interest in everything, and wanted to approve the smallest nomination or decision. He read extensively, particularly Ancient historians and Enlightenment philosophers, who inspired his reforms.

The pacification of society, however, could not be effective while some French citizens were considered 'undesirable'. That is why Napoleon offered an amnesty to the *émigrés*, many of whom came back to France, and decided to put an end to the persecution of Catholics. On the 15 July 1801, the Concordat was signed with the Holy See, which recognised Catholicism as the majority religion in France, but also granted religious freedom to other faiths. In order to better control the Church, however, Napoleon reserved the right to appoint the bishops.

Napoleon promised never to question the achievements of the Revolution, forgave enemies and gave compensation to the victims, and stabilised the situation through reforms that were almost unanimously accepted by the population. France seemed well on the way to national unity, although this was not quite yet the case.

Internal enemies

Although Napoleon managed to pacify the Vendée following the negotiations, he nonetheless remained the target of royalists who were determined to bring him down.

The entire balance of the current system relied on him alone: killing him would therefore mean overthrowing the regime and hopefully being able to reinstate the monarchy. This is why royalists, with the unexpected support of the British, became terrorists. On 24 December 1800, Napoleon narrowly escaped the plot of the rue Saint-Nicaise. He nonetheless spread the word that it was an attack committed by the Jacobins, which enabled him to get rid of the last agitators of the extreme left.

Three years later, a new conspiracy was uncovered. This time, the fault of the royalists was not only not denied, but a member of the Condé family of the House of Bourbon, the Duke of Enghien (1772-1804), was accused without proof of leading the plot. Captured in Germany, where he had fled to, he was summarily judged, condemned to death and executed on 21 March 1804 in the moat at Vincennes. The political impact of this event was clear, as it finally put an end to republicans' objections. On the other hand, it alienated royalists from Napoleon once and for all.

FOUCHÉ AND TALLEYRAND, NAPOLEON'S MINISTERS

The ruthless, regicidal revolutionary, Joseph Fouché (1759-1820) was the Minister of Police under the Consulate and the Empire. This political genius, who supported Napoleon during the 18 Brumaire coup, was frighteningly efficient, but did not back away from any crime. Disgraced several times for conspiring with the enemy, which was always remembered, he betrayed the Emperor again in 1814 and in 1815. Fouché's rival, Charles-Maurice de Talleyrand-Périgord (1754-1838), from an aristocratic background, was Minister of Foreign Affairs. This close advisor of the Emperor used his diplomatic skills to both serve and betray him, so that he could continue his political career under the Restoration. It was he who was famously described by Napoleon as "shit in a silk stocking" (Scurr, 2006).

The second Italian campaign

Almost as soon as he was named Consul, Napoleon went to fight in Italy, where the French were struggling against the Second Coalition that had formed in 1798. He first gathered a reserve army in Dijon in March 1800, before coming to the aid of General Masséna (1758-1817), who was under siege in Genoa by the Austrian army. In order to get there as quickly as possible and surprise the enemy, he crossed the Alps with difficulty via the Great St Bernard Pass, which had a reputation for being impossible to cross. Genoa fell, but he attacked the Austrians, overthrew their army, defeated them at Montebello and then definitively during the Battle of Marengo on 14 June 1800.

Napoleon Crossing the Alps, painting by Jacques-Louis David, 1801

This victory, following that of Moreau at Hohenlinden in Germany, led to the Treaty of Lunéville, which was signed with Austria in February 1801, and in which Austria accepted the French annexation of Switzerland, Belgium and the entire left bank of the Rhine, as well as most of its Italian territories. As French victories were commonplace, and the British minister William Pitt the Younger (1759-1806), a supporter of war, had resigned, Britain decided to sign the Treaty of Amiens on 25 March 1802. This agreement, despite being precarious, was a resounding success for Napoleon and was met with enthusiasm by the population. He had just accomplished one of the most important tasks that had been expected of him.

NAPOLEON I, THE EMPEROR

Why the Empire?

There were three main reasons for Napoleon and Joséphine's coronation in Notre-Dame cathedral in Paris, on 2 December 1804, with the benediction of Pope Pius VII. Firstly, peace had not lasted long. The British and the French had not ended up respecting the commitments made in Amiens, and hostilities began again in 1803. Napoleon realised that Britain would never accept French supremacy on the continent. A fight to the death broke out, directly or by proxy, and for which he needed his hands completely free. The Constitution of the Year XII, which instated the Empire, granted almost absolute power to the future Emperor.

Above all, it stated that "imperial dignity is hereditary" (Anderson, 1904). This aspect was the consequence of the many conspiracies that were contrived against the First Consul. Gradually, Napoleon became aware that everything he was building only depended on his life. Establishing inheritance would strengthen his work by guaranteeing that, even if he died, his succession was ensured. It was an attempt to dissociate the man from the new order of things, and discourage his enemies from attacking him once and for all. Failing to establish the Empire and its consequence, which was inheritance, meant risking a return to anarchy or to the

Ancien Régime with every attack against Napoleon. This is how the beneficiaries of the Revolution were convinced of the necessity of such a measure, which seemed so against the principles of 1792.

Additionally, Napoleon wanted to believe that by proclaiming the Empire, he would be better accepted by the European courts. The monarchies had been frightened by the French Revolution and its effects, which they saw as provocations: the execution of Louis XVI, the proclamation of the Republic and the propagation of its ideology through war. The Empire had to make them understand that the time of this revolution was over, that Napoleon was no longer their ideological enemy, and that peace could now be restored between people of the same world. However, he would never manage to be accepted by them.

PROPAGANDA THROUGH THE ARTS

Since the Consulate, Napoleon had understood the full advantage he could take of art to serve his ambitions. He ordered the great artists of his time to create works that beautifully depicted the main moments of his reign. This is why, among others, Jacques-Louis David (1748-1825) painted *Napoleon Crossing the Alps* (1800, Château de Malmaison), and made several copies intended for different powerful residences, and *Coronation of Napoleon and Joséphine* (1808, Louvre museum); Antoine-Jean Gros (1771-1835) painted *Bonaparte Visits the Plague Stricken in Jaffa* (1804,

Louvre museum) and *The Battle of Eylau* (1808, Louvre museum); while François Gérard (1770-1837) specialised in portraits, the most famous being *Napoleon I on his Imperial Throne*, in his coronation wear (1805, Musée de l'Armée). Napoleon also developed a powerful architectural style, inspired by Antiquity, as shown by the Arc de Triomphe (1806-1836) and the Vendôme Column (1806-1810), both built to commemorate his victory at Austerlitz (2 December 1805).

The Napoleonic saga

When the Third Coalition (1805) had been organised once again by Britain, Napoleon realised that he would have no respite until he defeated the British. He therefore prepared for a mass invasion of the British Isles, which his defeat at Trafalgar on 21 October 1805 made impossible. He therefore launched the *Grande Armée* against the British allies, won an initial victory against the Austrians in Ulm on 19 October 1805, before defeating Austro-Russian forces at Austerlitz. This battle, known as the Battle of the Three Emperors, as Napoleon was up against Alexander I of Russia and Francis II of Austria, was undoubtedly the finest, and tactically the best, of the Napoleonic era.

DID YOU KNOW?

It was at this battle that Napoleon said the famous words: "Soldiers: I am satisfied with you. [...] It will be enough for one of you to say, 'I was at the battle of Austerlitz;' for all your fellow citizens to exclaim, 'There is a brave man.'"

The victory at Austerlitz considerably weakened Austria and strengthened Napoleon's supremacy, and he reorganised the Empire. He notably joined the German states into the Confederation of the Rhine, to the detriment of Prussia, who at that time were part of the Fourth Coalition against France (1806-1807). It only took Napoleon three weeks to occupy Berlin, after wiping out Prussian forces in Jena on 14 October 1806. He then seized Poland, where he was welcomed as a liberator – as Russia and Prussia had divided the country between them in 1793 – and then began to pursue the Russians, whom he forced to confront him at the Battle of Eylau on 8 February 1807. For the first time, victory did not come easily, and it would not be until the definitive victory at the Battle of Friedland four months later that the Treaty of Tilsit, an alliance treaty between France and Russia whose main provision was the closure of Russian ports to British trade, was signed, on 7 July 1807. This was proof that, even in the Eastern plains or against the Russians, it was always really Britain that Napoleon was fighting against.

Thus, at the end of 1806, Napoleon decreed a continental blockade, whose effects began to be felt seriously on the British Isles. The British tried incessantly to break it, from the North and the South. This is why they tried to form alliances with Spain and Portugal, and it was to counter this eventuality that Napoleon decided to take control of the Iberian Peninsula in 1808. The Spanish episode, however, was disastrous, and marked the start of the decline of Napoleon's Empire. Two main factors explain this phenomenon: a profoundly Catholic Iberian population, violently hostile towards the French due to the French Revolution; and a new type of fighting, guerrilla warfare, which the French marshals had to confront, left to their own devices and giving their enemies free reign.

The painting entitled *The Third of May 1808* (1814, Prado Museum) by the painter Francisco Goya (1746-1828) depicts the execution, on 3 May 1808, of the Spanish prisoners captured by French troops during the revolt of 2 May in Madrid.

At the same time, with an army composed mainly of new recruits and foreign auxiliaries, as the veterans were in Spain, Napoleon had to rush to the Eastern front to fight a Fifth Coalition (April-October 1809), encouraged by his setbacks in the Iberian Peninsula. The campaign ended in a victory, during the Battle of Wagram on 6 July 1809, but the Empire was weakened. Napoleon became fed up of the double game being played by Alexander I, and although the two Empires were allies, he decided to invade Russia during the summer of 1812 with all 450 000 men from the *Grande Armée*.

The French won the Battle of Borodino on 7 September 1812, but the losses were great and the consequences limited, as the Russian army was not destroyed. Napoleon went after the army, led by General Kutuzov (1745-1813) who was tactically evasive, even going as far as abandoning Moscow, which the French occupied on 14 September 1812. Judging the situation to be precarious, Napoleon therefore decided to retreat. This retreat, under the attack of winter and the harassment of the Russian army, much like the retreat from the Battle of Berezina in November 1812, was a disaster. Napoleon hurriedly returned to Paris.

DOWNFALL

The Russian campaign, which ended in a total defeat and had cost the lives of 200 000 French soldiers and 300 000 Russians, emboldened Napoleon's enemies, who formed a Sixth Coalition (1812-1814), this time comprising Austria, which was nonetheless still linked to Napoleon through his wife, Marie-Louise. Following defeat in Leipzig, he had to abandon Germany, then Holland, and withdraw into France. Spain had already been lost in June 1813. At the start of 1814, despite the victories in the French campaign, Napoleon was unable to repel his enemies and, withdrawn to Fontainebleau, abdicated on 4 April 1814.

Napoleon at Fontainebleau, 31 March 1814, painting by Paul Delaroche, 1840.

Paradoxically, from 1813 to 1814, Napoleon won more battles than he lost. However, he did not manage to reap the benefits of his victories. There are various reasons for this, but most of them involve his enemies' determination, as their populations were being won over by a nationalism that had been spreading since the early 1800s, and the general discouragement of Napoleon's army, whose officers unwillingly carried out the Emperor's orders, or indeed simply refused to carry them out at all. Some even betrayed him, notably the auxiliary bodies made up of foreign troops, who sometimes turned against him in the middle of a battle. In addition, it was these generals who forced Napoleon to abdicate.

The Emperor was then exiled to the island of Elba, where he was authorised to reign alone. He was unable, however, at the age of 45, to be content with such a kingdom and, deceiving the British, landed in France on 1 March 1815 with around a thousand men. He reputation was such that he was cheered the whole way, and all the armies sent to fight against him ended up storming Paris by his side, such as Marshal Ney (1769-1815), who had rejoined the Bourbons in 1814, and who had promised to bring Napoleon back to Louis XVIII in an iron cage.

In Paris, however, everything had changed. The court had disappeared and many former important figures of the Empire had followed Louis XVIII into exile. Napoleon was apathetic, ill-at-ease and morose. In order to be accepted, he promised to behave like a constitutional monarch and to keep the chambers instated by Louis XVIII's charter, but this constraint on his power was tiresome, particularly when he needed his hands completely free to fight the Seventh Coalition (March-June 1815), which had soon formed following his return.

The decisive battle took place at Waterloo on 18 June 1815. The enemy armies were led by the Duke of Wellington (1769-1852) for the British, and Blücher (1742-1819) for the Prussians. Rarely could a battle have been so crucial: winning would mean forcing the coalition members to negotiate and returning to Paris in a position of strength; losing would mean finally bidding farewell to power, which Napoleon had regained almost miraculously three months earlier. A series of tactical errors, underestimating the enemy and inexperienced troops were the main causes of this final defeat, which led to Napoleon's second abdication on 22 June 1815.

Napoleon, who refused to commit the dishonour of fleeing, handed himself over to the British and was soon sent to Saint Helena, as it was feared that his glory would continue to ignite passions. Even in exile in the middle of nowhere, he was still a threat to the Allies, and had to endure the harassment of his British gaoler. He then began to entrust

his reflections on his life to the loved ones who had accom-
panied him and almost all of whom kept diaries, the most
famous being Emmanuel de Las Cases (1766-1842). But
they all ended up leaving the island one after another, and
Napoleon was practically alone when he died on 5 May 1821.

IMPACT

POLITICAL LEGACY

Even before his death, Napoleon was the main reference point of the 19th century, whether people aligned themselves with him or opposed him. He was behind the major ideology of Bonapartism, which dominated the political history of the century, and whose range was so vast that it gained the support of both the left and the right. Everything depended on what was retained from Napoleon's 20 years in power. For some, the most important thing was the confirmation of the Revolution's achievements; for others, it was the personality of this man who owed what he had become to himself alone. Others valued France's greatness and domination of Europe. Everyone appreciated the advantages of strong power derived from popular legitimacy. Napoleon managed to achieve continuity between the Ancien Régime and the Revolution, to the extent that we owe him for reviving one and saving the other.

Being a Bonapartist meant rising above political parties, notably the two main movements that structured French political life in the 19th century: royalism and republicanism. This is how Louis-Napoleon Bonaparte, Napoleon's nephew and future Napoleon III, presented himself. Although the Second Empire (1852-1870) began with a coup d'état, it nonetheless gained the support of the majority of French citizens, who hoped to find a fantasy golden age with its help. As its fall was not political, but military, Bonapartism remained popular until the end of the Second Empire.

However, the death of Napoleon III's son in 1879, the conflicts that this led to between his various potential successors at the head of the family, and the stability of the Third Republic (1870-1940), which was supported by many Bonapartists, signalled the political decline of this ideology.

The administrative and institutional work of Napoleon survived beyond revolutions, political regimes and wars. Many of the institutions he set up still exist today, and the Napoleonic Code, although it has been reworked, is still used. Much of the administrative centralisation of France was realised under the Empire. More generally, Napoleon was behind the French attraction to what we call the 'great man', which General de Gaulle (1890-1970) would take advantage of during the Second World War (1939-1945) and the establishment of the Fifth Republic. Even today, politicians have a tendency to tackle this.

THE NAPOLEONIC LEGEND

Aside from Napoleon's concrete achievements and their longevity, it is the extraordinary fate of this man that has fascinated people for two centuries. He was no stranger to having such an impact. From the First Italian Campaign, he skilfully orchestrated his legend, raising his battle feats into epic tales, and insisting on his connections with the great men of the past, Alexander the Great, Charlemagne (742/747-814) or the French monarchs. The memoirs of Saint Helena, which would be published by Emmanuel de Las Cases under the title *The Memorial of Saint Helena*, constituted the defining moment of the myth's construction.

This portrayal of himself would have been impossible, however, if it had not had an unusual life as its basis. Coming from almost nothing and reaching dizzying heights in human society, he abruptly found himself excluded from the world. It did seem, however, that the responsibility for this downfall was less due to human actions than to fate, a sentiment that gave rise to the eminently romantic figure of Napoleon. Nor could we forget the man's personality. Even at the highest point of his power, he always demonstrated austerity in his daily life, closeness to people, particularly to his soldiers, and temperance in the management of his various matters, all of which would significantly contribute to creating his myth: an Emperor who ruled almost all of Europe in a grey coat and undecorated bicorn hat.

Indeed, Napoleon always maintained the simplicity of his environment. He held on to the memories of a time when he had only been an officer-in-training, recipient of a royal scholarship and had spoken French with a thick Corsican accent. It is undoubtedly this aspect of his life that fascinates us the most nowadays. He perfectly embodies the 'self-made man', who frees himself from his initial situation and manages to establish himself among the elite of his time using only his own qualities. He took control of his own destiny. By doing so, Napoleon acted as a precursor to the modern world and can still be a model for contemporary society, despite its being less and less susceptible to long reigns such as his and the large number of critical works about him that have appeared over the last 40 years.

CONTEMPORARY RE-ENACTMENTS

The bicentenary of Napoleon's battles, which involved all of Europe and which continue to interest people today, was an opportunity for large commemorative re-enactments. The largest ever undertaken in Europe, that of Waterloo, which took place between 18 and 21 June 2015, involved 5000 actors, 300 horses, 100 canons and over 200 000 spectators.

SUMMARY

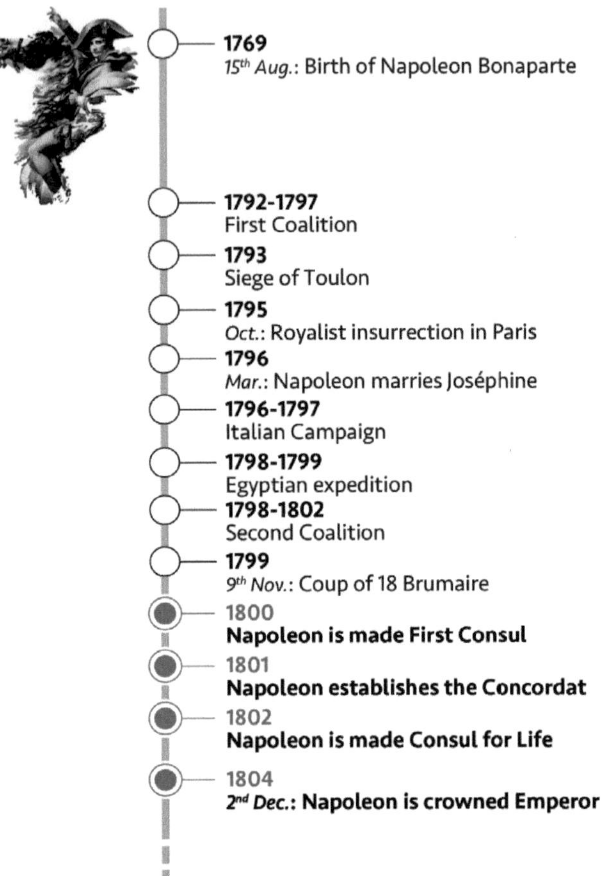

1769
15th Aug.: Birth of Napoleon Bonaparte

1792-1797
First Coalition

1793
Siege of Toulon

1795
Oct.: Royalist insurrection in Paris

1796
Mar.: Napoleon marries Joséphine

1796-1797
Italian Campaign

1798-1799
Egyptian expedition

1798-1802
Second Coalition

1799
9th Nov.: Coup of 18 Brumaire

1800
Napoleon is made First Consul

1801
Napoleon establishes the Concordat

1802
Napoleon is made Consul for Life

1804
2nd Dec.: **Napoleon is crowned Emperor**

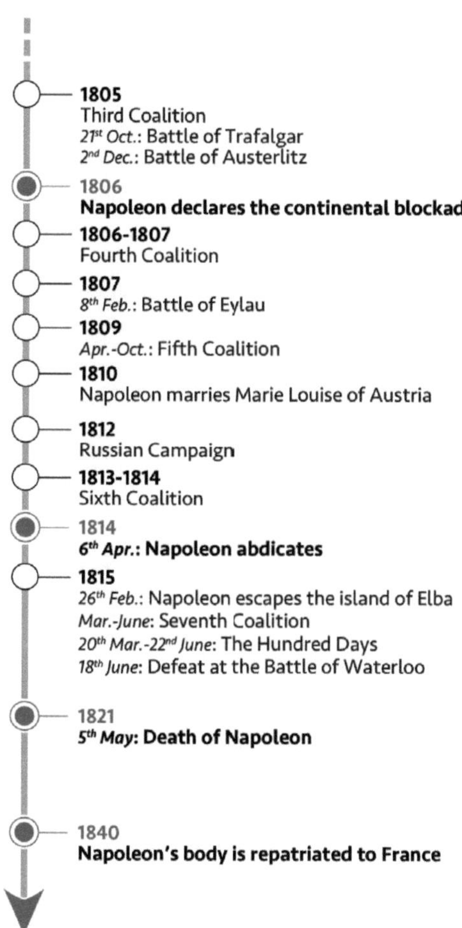

- Napoleon Bonaparte was made a general in 1795, named First Consul in 1800, following the coup d'état of

18 Brumaire, and crowned Emperor on 2 December 1804.

- Napoleon's major victories were those of Lodi and Arcole during the First Italian Campaign (1796-1797); the Pyramids and Abu Qir during the Egypt campaign (1798-1799); Marengo during the second Italian campaign (1800); Ulm and Austerlitz (1805) against the Austrians and the Russians; Jena, Eylau and Friedland (1807) against the Prussians and the Russians; and Wagram (1809) against the Austrians.

- His main defeats were at Trafalgar (1805) against the British and Waterloo (1815) against the Allies, as well as his retreat from Russia (1812). Before that, the expedition to Egypt in 1798-1799 had ended in military failure, but scientific success.

- From 1800 onwards, the fundamental aim of all of Napoleon's campaigns was to be victorious against the British. To this end, he established the continental blockade, which meant that he required control over all of Europe's maritime borders, either through alliances or through annexations.

- Politically, Napoleon tried to reconcile the French by protecting the moral and material achievements of the Revolution on the one hand, and compensating the victims on the other.

- The creation of the prefects, the Bank of France, higher education in France, the National Order of the Legion of Honour, the *franc germinal* and the Civil Code are all due to Napoleon.

- The Concordat, which re-established relations between France and the papacy, was signed on 15 July 1801.

- The attacks made on Napoleon, the threat of the

European coalitions and the desire to be done with the Revolution led to the Empire and its main consequence, the inheritance of the title of Emperor.

- Very skilled in propaganda, Napoleon himself was behind his legends, which he wrote during his conquests and his main achievements, and which culminated in the publication of *The Memorial of Saint Helena*.

We want to hear from you!
Leave a comment on your online library
and share your favourite books on social media!

FIND OUT MORE

BIBLIOGRAPHY

- Anderson, F. M. (1904) *The Constitutions and Other Select Documents Illustrative of the History of France, 1789-1901*. Minneapolis: H. W. Wilson.
- Bainville, J. (1933) *Napoléon*. Paris: Plon.
- Benoist-Méchin, J. (1978) *Bonaparte en Égypte ou le rêve inassouvi*. Paris: Perrin.
- Castelot, A. (1999) *Napoléon*. Paris: Perrin.
- Gueniffey, P. (2013) *Bonaparte: 1769-1802*. Paris: Gallimard.
- Lentz, T. (2004) *Napoléon*. Paris: Presses universitaires de France.
- Scurr, R. (2006) He quipped while Napoleon quaked. *The Telegraph*. [Online]. [Accessed 19 January 2017]. Available from: <http://www.telegraph.co.uk/culture/books/3657043/He-quipped-while-Napoleon-quaked.html>
- Tarbell, I. M. (1896) *Napoleon's Addresses: Selections from the Proclamations, Speeches and Correspondence of Napoleon Bonaparte*. Boston: Joseph Knight.
- Tulard, J. (1987) *Napoléon ou le mythe du sauveur*. Paris: Fayard.

ADDITIONAL SOURCES

- Cornwell, B. (2016) *Waterloo: The History of Four Days, Three Armies and Three Battles*. New York: Harper.
- Nafziger, G. F. (2015) *The End of Empire: Napoleon's 1814*

Campaign. Solihull: Helion & Company.
- Roberts, A. (2015) *Napoleon: A Life*. New York: Penguin Books.

ICONOGRAPHIC SOURCES

- Watercolour by Berthault depicting the attack on the National Convention of 13 Vendémiaire Year 4. Royalty-free reproduction picture.
- *Napoleon leaving Elba*, on 26 February 1815, painting by Joseph Beaume, 1836. Royalty-free reproduction picture.
- *Bonaparte at the Council of Five Hundred*, in Saint-Cloud, on 10 November 1799, painting by François Bouchot, 1840. Royalty-free reproduction picture.
- *The Battle of Lodi*, painting by Louis-François Lejeune, 1804. Royalty-free reproduction picture.
- Painting depicting the Battle of the Pyramids. Royalty-free reproduction picture.
- *Napoleon Crossing the Alps*, painting by Jacques-Louis David, 1801. Royalty-free reproduction picture.
- *The Third of May 1808*, painting by Francisco Goya, 1814. Royalty-free reproduction picture.
- *Napoleon at Fontainebleau*, 31 March 1814, painting by Paul Delaroche, 1840. Royalty-free reproduction picture.

IMPROVE YOUR GENERAL KNOWLEDGE
IN A BLINK OF AN EYE !

www.50minutes.com